Marvelous Migration

by Lara Bove

PEARSON

Scott
Foresman

Editorial Offices: Glenview, Illinois • Parsippany, New Jersey • New York, New York
Sales Offices: Needham, Massachusetts • Duluth, Georgia • Glenview, Illinois
Coppell, Texas • Ontario, California • Mesa, Arizona

Opener: Getty Images, Corbis; 1 Corbis; 3 Corbis; 5 Getty Images; 6 Getty Images; 8 Corbis; 9 ImageWorks; 10 Animals Animals/Earth Scenes; 11 Photo Researchers, Gerlach Nature Photography, Image Researchers; 13 ©DK Images; 14 Animals Animals/Earth Scenes; 15 Getty Images; 16 Color-Pic, Inc.; 17 Minden Pictures, Animals Animals/Earth Scenes, Color-Pic, Inc.; 18 Photo Researchers, ©DK Images, Corbis

ISBN: 0-328-13446-5

6 7 8 9 10 V0G1 14 13 12 11 10 09 08 07

Animals That Migrate

Have you ever heard the phrase "birds fly south for the winter"? This is an example of migration.

Many animals migrate. They move around during their lives. They may live in one place during the spring. Then they move somewhere else in the winter.

They might be born in one place, but then they move away to a different place. When they are ready to have babies, they go back to the place where they were born.

This book describes how caribou, bats, and monarch butterflies migrate. It also tells why they migrate.

A herd of caribou

A Different Kind of Deer

Caribou are a type of deer. They are also called reindeer. They live in the coldest part of North America, in the Arctic, and they are mammals. One characteristic that makes this type of deer special is that both males and females have antlers. No other female deer has antlers.

The ground in the Arctic is mostly barren. Very little grows there. Barren ground caribou live in **massive** herds. There are around 500,000 in the largest herd. The males stand three to five feet tall, and they can weigh up to six hundred pounds. Imagine the **rumbling** sound they must make when they run.

Caribou on the run

Caribou Migration

These animals live in the tundra in the spring. There are no trees in the tundra because of the strong winds and cold weather. The ground is always frozen, but in summer the top layer melts a little. Green grass and small plants grow, and many birds and insects live there.

In June the cows, or the female caribou, give birth to calves. Most of the cows in a herd give birth during the same two weeks.

Summer is short in the Arctic. When summer starts to end in July, the caribou migrate south for the winter. They go to the *taiga*, or the evergreen forest. The caribou stay there until the end of winter. Then they move back to the tundra for the summer. The cycle begins again.

Why Migrate?

Caribou do not go to the exact same place each spring and fall. Barren ground caribou go to the Arctic each spring, and they go to the taiga each winter. They do not travel to the same mountain, though. Their migration depends on where they find food.

Caribou in the snow of Alaska

The caribou eat different food in the winter and summer. They eat lichen in the winter. Reindeer moss is one kind. It grows under the snow. It is bushy, has many branches, and grows close to the ground. Caribou can smell it under the snow. Then they use their hooves to dig it out. Sometimes they will dig two feet deep to find it. More plants grow in the summer, such as flower buds and grass, and caribou can eat many of them.

The caribou also travel to stay away from predators, such as wolves. Wolves have pups in the spring, but most will not bring their young to the tundra. The tundra has fewer wolves in the spring, which makes it safer for the caribou.

Mosquitoes bother caribou in the summer, taking a quart of the caribou's blood each week. This makes the caribou slower and weaker. The caribou try to find a breeze, they wade in water, or they stand close together to avoid being bitten by those pesky mosquitoes! In August it gets colder and the mosquitoes die out.

A Bat's Wing

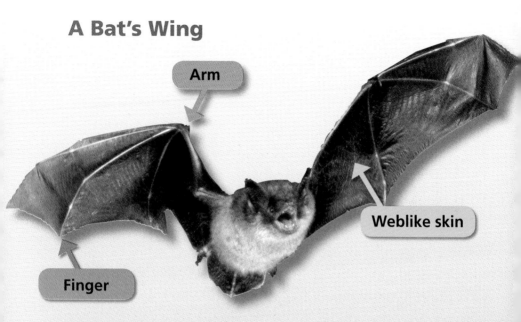

Arm

Weblike skin

Finger

Bats

Bats also migrate. Some people think bats are scary animals. Others think they are wonderful. Bats are mammals that can fly. Like other mammals, such as the caribou, bats have fur. They give birth to live animals and feed their babies with mother's milk.

Bats have hands and feet. Their hands and fingers are very large compared to their small bodies. They have weblike skin between their fingers, making wings. This skin extends to their arms and down their bodies to their legs. Bats use their fingers to help them fly. Moving their fingers together and apart helps them fly in different directions.

Bats also like to hang upside down. They spend a lot of time grooming themselves in this position. They hold on to a branch or cliff with one foot. Then they use the other foot to clean themselves.

Bats live all over the world. Mexican free-tailed bats migrate between Mexico and Texas. These **tropical** bats eat insects. One large group lives in Austin, Texas, in the summer. Many of them fly near the Congress Avenue bridge. They will eat up to thirty thousand pounds of insects every night. One bat can catch six hundred mosquitoes in an hour. That's a lot of bugs!

A hoary bat hangs upside down.

People watch the bats at the Congress Avenue bridge in Austin, Texas.

Mexican free-tailed
bats fly out of a cave.

In the winter the Mexican free-tailed bats fly south to Mexico. They stay there until the spring. Then many of the bats move back to Texas. The females go to special nursery caves. Here they give birth to their young. The newborn bats live in these caves. The mothers come to the caves to care for them and to feed them milk.

Other bats, such as the silver-haired bat, hoary bat, and red bat, migrate to the northern United States and Canada in the spring. The silver-haired bat winters in the southern United States. The hoary bat and the red bat spend their winters in Central America.

Silver-haired bat

Hoary bat

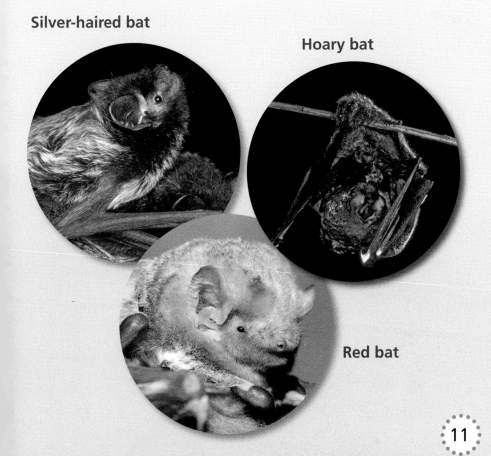

Red bat

Creatures of the Night

All bats are nocturnal. This means they are asleep during the day and awake at night. This may help bats live longer because many predators are sleeping at night. Bats can live from ten to twenty years!

Some bats use sound to help them hunt for food at night. First, the bat makes a noise. When the sound waves hit an object, the sound bounces back to the bat, similar to an echo. Then the bat can figure out the location of the object. Bats can also tell the size of the object. They can figure out if it is a mosquito or a large bug.

Bats use sound to help them find more than just food. They also want to know if there is anything they might fly into!

How Bats Find Food

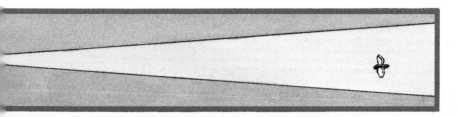

At night, when a bat is hunting,
it sends out sound waves.

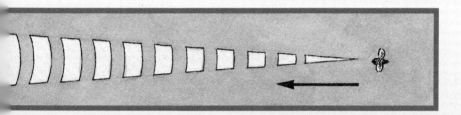

The sound waves bounce off the insect.

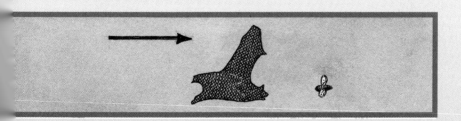

The echo of the sound helps
the bat catch its prey.

Monarch Butterflies

Monarch butterflies are not mammals. They are insects, and like the caribou and bats, they migrate too. In late summer, monarch butterflies begin their winter migration. They fly south to California or Mexico. They stop to eat nectar along the way. In fact, the butterflies gain weight while they travel, but they do not stop for long during their journey. They do not want to get caught in the cold winter climate of the north. They cannot fly if they get too cold.

Monarch butterflies travel far. They fly about two thousand miles each fall and spring. They fly over **lagoons,** and they have even flown over large sections of the Gulf of Mexico.

Winter Sites

Monarch butterflies go to the exact same place each winter. The creatures who fly south were born in the north. How do butterflies know where to go? Scientists still cannot answer this question.

One place the butterflies spend the winter is on the coast of California. California's coast has many **bluffs.** These steep cliffs help create fog. The butterflies get water from streams and foggy air, which keeps them from drying out. Others migrate to the mountains of Mexico.

Monarch butterflies gather together on a tree in Mexico.

Moving North

The days get longer and warmer at the end of winter. The butterflies move around more. They begin mating and then fly north in March.

When they get there, they look for milkweed plants on which to lay their eggs. The eggs hatch into caterpillars that eat the milkweed and create a cocoon. Two weeks later a butterfly hatches.

These monarch butterflies will live in the north during the summer. Each female lays hundreds of eggs. Summer monarchs live only about three to five weeks, but the total number of monarch butterflies rises all summer long. In late fall the cycle begins again.

Step 1

Monarch butterflies lay their eggs on milkweed leaves. This is the only leaf that the monarch caterpillars can eat. The milkweed is poisonous to birds and other predators. It helps protect the monarch butterfly.

The eggs hatch into caterpillars. The caterpillar eats milkweed and grows.

The caterpillar makes a cocoon. It stays inside of this for about two weeks.

The monarch butterfly comes out of the cocoon. It will soon lay eggs on the milkweed.

Some **biologists,** or scientists who study living things, study the migration patterns of animals. Here are some tools they use to study them.

Radio collars

These bands are put on the animal's neck, like this one on a cow elk. They send a radio signal. The biologists use the signal to track the animal's movements.

Maps and diagrams

The researchers track the data. Then they chart it on a map to make a diagram. This map shows the summer and winter migration routes of the monarch butterfly.

Butterfly tags

These tags are placed on butterflies' wings. School children and other volunteers catch butterflies and put on the tags. Now scientists can track where these tagged butterflies travel.

Caribou, bats, and monarch butterflies are just three of the many creatures that migrate from place to place during their lifetimes. It is amazing how these creatures know when to migrate and where to travel, but somehow they do! Migration is part of their survival. Each year the cycle begins again, and each year the journey continues.

Monarch butterflies
- are insects
- travel to the same place each winter
- lay eggs in the spring
- hatch as caterpillars

- live in Canada during the summer

Caribou
- live in the Arctic
- live in massive herds
- migrate to different places
- eat lichen

- migrate north in summer and south in winter

- spend winters in Mexico
- eat nectar

- are mammals

Bats
- eat insects
- sleep during the day
- live 10–20 years

Glossary

biologists *n.* scientists who study living things, including their origins, structures, activities, and distribution.

bluffs *n.* high, steep slopes or cliffs.

lagoons *n.* ponds or small lakes, especially ones connected with a larger body of water.

massive *adj.* big and heavy; bulky.

rumbling *adj.* making deep, heavy, continuous sound.

tropical *adj.* of or like the regions 23.45 degrees north and south of the equator where the sun can shine directly overhead.